The Institute that became an Institution

The History of the Royal Albert Institute and its Trust

with a Foreword by
HRH The Prince Philip, Duke of Edinburgh,
KG, KT, OM, GBE, AC, QSO, PC

and a Preface by
Mr Peter Gray MBE, Chairman of the Trustees

The Institute that became an Institution
*The History of the Royal Albert Institute
and its Trust*

Second edition, fully revised 2016

Copyright © John E Handcock

The rights of John E Handcock to be identified as the Authors of this work have been asserted by him in accordance with the Copyright, Designs and Patents Act 1988.

All rights reserved.
No part of this book may be reprinted or reproduced or utilised in any form or by any electronic, mechanical or other means, now known or hereafter invented, including photocopying and recording, or in any information storage retrieval system, nor transmitted in any form or by any means without the permission in writing from the Author.

ISBN 9780954587116

Cover design by Nedula Graphics
Layout by Cidixith at STP

Although every precaution has been taken in the preparation of this book, the publisher and authors assume no responsibility for errors or omissions. Neither is any liability assumed for damages resulting from the use of this information contained herein.

A catalogue record for this book is available from the British Library.

Printed by SSMedia, Rickmansworth

The Institute that became an Institution

*The History of the Royal Albert Institute
and its Trust*

by
John E Handcock CVO, DL, LL.B

ALBERT MEMORIAL

The photographs and illustrations used in this work are primarily from the private collections of John E Handcock and Carol Dixon-Smith. To the best of their knowledge and except as indicated below, any other images used are in the public domain.

The photograph of the institute in 1890 is used with the kind permission of the Royal Windsor Website www.thamesweb.co.uk

The two photographs of the removal of Prince Albert's statue were used with the kind permission of Mr E Kupfermann.

Contents

Foreword
*HRH Prince Philip, The Duke of Edinburgh
KG, KT, OM, GBE, AC, QSO, PC*

Preface
Peter Gray MBE, Chairman of the Trustees

Acknowledgements

Chapter	*Page*
1. December 1866	2
2. January 1880	6
3. Art is universal	7
4. Visitors	9
5. Moving Forward	12
6. A New Vision	14
7. The Trust	17
8. Into and Beyond the 21st Century	32
Appendix	34
Bibliography	35
Index	36

Foreword

BUCKINGHAM PALACE

One of the clues to the vitality of a community is evidence of communal pride and the willingness of its members to support local initiatives. The Royal Albert Institute Trust is just such an organisation. Set up in memory of Prince Albert, it continues to make a significant contribution to the intellectual and social life in the Royal Borough.

The author deserves great credit for compiling this account of the activities and initiatives of the Trust. He has created *a record of its achievements which, I have no doubt, future generations* will treasure.

Philip

The Institute 1880

Preface

Like many others who spent their teenage years in Windsor, I remember 'The Institute' as everybody called it. Known mainly for the dances they organised on Saturday evening, I sometimes wondered what happened there the rest of the week. Many years later I was invited to become a Trustee of the present Trust and at last found out a lot of facts about it, and about the building in Sheet Street.

Most, if not all of this knowledge, was passed on to me by John Handcock who has been Clerk to the Trustees since 1966. This book, as any book or article written by John, is full of fact and detail, and is a pleasure to read.

John Handcock is himself 'an institution' and probably knows more about Windsor than anyone else I know. Having read and enjoyed reading this book, and learned many more things about the early days, I recommend it to you.

Peter Gray MBE
Chairman of the Trustees

In the 1890s

The Royal Albert Institute

In the 1960s   *In the 1970s*

Moving Romanelli's Prince Albert Statute

*Above:
Onlookers watch as the statue is carefully moved to safety after being lifted from the building*

*Left:
The statue is inspected for damage and weathering before being packed and moved into temporary storage*

Acknowledgements

The author is especially grateful to His Royal Highness, The Prince Philip, Duke of Edinburgh, for his kindness in reading the first edition of this book, and for his correction of the entry in the Visitors' Book relating to the Prince and Princess of Battenberg, Grandparents of His Royal Highness (rectified in this second edition). The author is, moreover, especially appreciative of the foreword which His Royal Highness has generously written for this book.

The author's appreciation also goes to Mr Peter Grey MBE, for kindly contributing the Preface. He also wishes to express his thanks to his secretary, Karen Drury, for her patient grappling with his handwriting, her meticulous typing and her very helpful suggestions.

His thanks and gratitude go to his daughter, Nicola Handcock, for proofreading the final draft and particularly to Peggy, his wife, for so graciously excusing him from numerous household chores during the compilation of this book.

Appreciation is also due to Carol Dixon-Smith for her expertise in seeing this work through to its ultimate publication, and to Rebecca Heaton for her expert work on the cover design.

December 1866

When Francis Charles Augustus Albert Emmanuel, Prince of Saxe-Coburg and Gotha, and Consort of Queen Victoria, died prematurely aged forty two, at Windsor Castle on 14th December 1861 in the same room where William IV expired, it was inevitable, given the widespread grief, that memorials in many forms would swiftly proliferate throughout the land.

In Windsor, a golden opportunity presented itself to honour the memory of the Prince Consort. There had existed in the town since 1835 a Literary Scientific and Mechanics Institute for the propagation of literature and music similar to a multitude of such bodies in many towns created for the educational enlightenment of skilled manual workers and artisans. They were regarded by some as fostering revolutionary ideals, although this was by no means a universal condemnation. At a meeting on 3rd December 1866, the Trustees of the Institute resolved to erect a new building to be called the Albert Institute to comprise

> *amongst other necessary rooms, a Commodious Lecture Hall capable of holding at least 500 persons and to name it* The Albert Institute.

Such a choice of name was imaginative and appropriate. Through his twenty years at the Queen's side, Prince Albert had energetically espoused a cornucopia of cultural activities, not the least of which was the cause of educational reform and expansion. It was he, for example, who was much involved with the foundation of Wellington College in 1856. His artistic and scientific interests were eclectic and wide ranging. At Windsor he instigated the building of the Royal Dairy, and in 1850 he formed the Royal Society for the Improvement of the Conditions of the Labouring Classes which led to housing improvements and the building of Prince Consort Cottages.

The Royal Dairy at Frogmore

December 1866

In 1847 the Windsor & Eton Choral Society, founded ten years earlier, made him their first patron.

According to the stimulating, if iconoclastic, historian A N Wilson, Prince Albert's arrival in England *'brought qualities of seriousness and intelligence to public life which are almost without parallel '* and later he describes the Prince as an

> *accomplished musician and linguist, good art historian, amateur architect, politically aware, liberal in religion and politics, intelligently abreast of contemporary scientific discovery.*

No better name for the fledgling Institute could have been devised.

Such is the background to the creation of the Albert Institute, the original endowment of which was set up by a Conveyance dated 31st December 1867, whereby the Great Western Railway Company conveyed two plots of land in Sheet Street, Windsor, on which formerly stood the Royal Mews, to twenty three Trustees for the sum of £600. On 3rd June 1869, the Trustees settled the same piece of land for the purpose of the Windsor & Eton Literary, Scientific and Mechanics Institution.

The Building Committee, whose Secretary was Mr Frank Buckland, encountered serious difficulties. As with those of Prince Albert himself in spear-heading the Great Exhibition of 1851, they were mainly financial. In 1870 fresh efforts, probably inspired by a stinging attack from the local paper, resulted in a flurry of donations from some of the more affluent members and one of £50 from the Queen herself. Thereafter the Building Committee engaged in a new surge of enthusiasm, evidently imbued with the spirit of Winston Churchill, *'Don't take no for an answer. Never submit to failure'* as enunciated in *My Early Life*. Thereafter the project prospered, the foundation stone being laid in March 1879 by Prince Christian, the husband of the Queen's fourth daughter. The Queen herself occasionally visited the site to inspect the progress of the works, and that she regarded the Institute with royal favour was evidenced by the grant of the '*Royal*' prefix.

HRH Prince Christian

December 1866

On 10th January, amid scenes of jubilation, the new and very handsome building was opened by the Prince of Wales.

We are told that the Institute

> contains Reading and Class-rooms, Lending Library, Gymnasium, a large Hall for Concerts, Lectures, Balls, capable of holding upwards of five hundred persons, rooms for Science and Art Classes and connections with South Kensington, a Museum of local and other objects of interest.

The building had a frontage to Sheet Street of seventy feet and was constructed in the late Tudor style, harmonising with other Windsor buildings, and was of red brick with stone dressings and mullions with reddish brown roof tiles. The total cost was some £ 6,000 of which, at the time of opening, £2,500 remained to be raised. The architects were Messrs H F Bacon and E Ingress Bell of London.

As befitted the magnificence of the edifice, there was positioned in a niche over the main entrance a splendid marble statue of Prince Albert in the robes of a Knight of the Garter, sculpted by Signor Romanelli of Florence and donated by Mrs Richardson-Gardner, wife of the town's Member of Parliament. This statue, from fear of exposure to the weather, was later replaced in its elevated niche by a stone replica, the original being moved to the large hall. When the building was sold and redeveloped more than eighty years later, both marble and stone statues were damaged by vandals. After expert repair by Mr John Gough, a local architect, they were presented by the Trustees to the Royal Borough. The Romanelli marble statue was subsequently placed on loan in the vestibule to Holy Trinity Church, and the stone replacement was loaned to the new owners, The Windsor Life Assurance Company, and reinstated in its original niche which was incorporated into the redeveloped building.

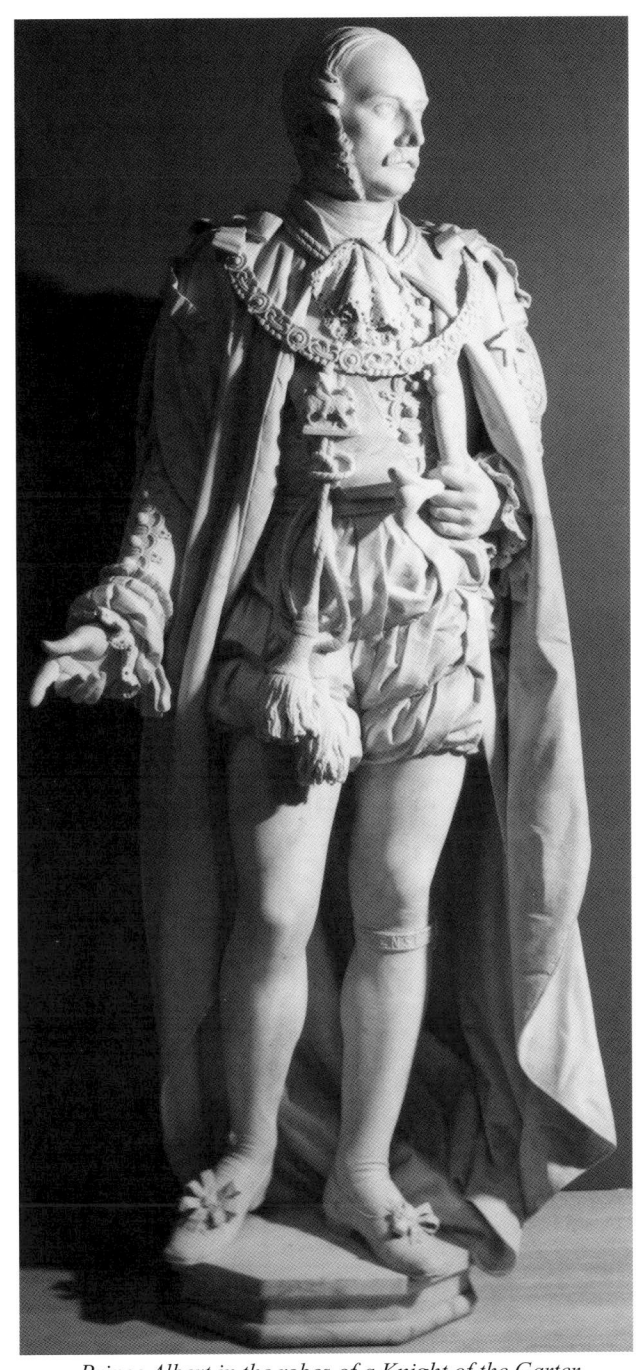
Prince Albert in the robes of a Knight of the Garter
(Sculpted by Signor Romanelli of Florence)

January 1880

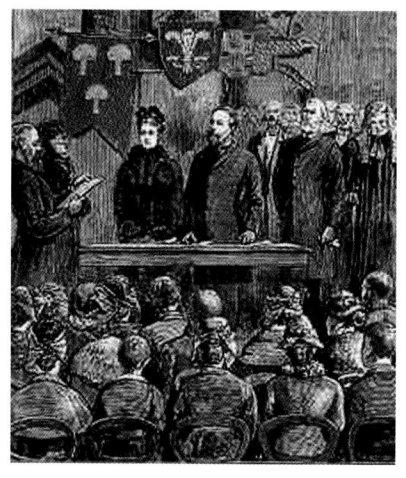

The opening ceremony on 10th January 1880 was of sufficient import to merit a glowing report in the Illustrated London News which recorded the names of the Building Committee (in addition to the Secretary) as the Revd. F J Rawlins, Dr Fairbank, Captain Bulkeley, Sir George Elvey, Mr R Richardson-Gardner, Mr Drew of Eton College, and the Mayor of Windsor, Mr John Webb, (whose unrelated namesake curiously became Mayor of the Royal Borough of Windsor & Maidenhead in Millennium Year 2000). The journal also depicted fine engravings of the *'imposing facade'* of the building and of the royal opening. The Prince of Wales was accompanied by the Prince and Princess of Schleswig-Holstein, he at that time living at Cumberland Lodge as Ranger of Windsor Great Park. The royal personages were received by the Bishop of Oxford, the Rt. Revd. Bishop Mackarness and the Dean of Windsor, the Hon. and the Very Revd. Gerald Wellesley, nephew of the Duke of Wellington and a sagacious and trusted confidant of the Queen.

The ceremony was enlivened by the combined choirs of St George's Chapel and Eton College, together with the string band of the 2nd Lifeguards, who performed a special cantata, composed by Sir George Elvey, the organist of St George's Chapel. The Prince of Wales received an address to which he made *'a suitable reply'* and the Bishop gave the Blessing. That evening the members of the Building Committee held a well-deserved supper at the Castle Hotel presided over by Dr Fairbank, whose sudden death about four weeks later was a great loss to the Committee, although he died in the knowledge that he had successfully fought the good fight.

The Royal Albert Institute was in business and only four days later on 14th January the first concert took place with a ball following in the evening.

Art is universal

Princess Christian

Jenny Lind

Sir Edward Elgar

The new venture rapidly became a focus for an ever increasing expansion of the town's cultural life. For the populace, concerts were undoubtedly the main magnet. Mr Thomas Dyson, who came to Windsor as a Lay Clerk in 1854 and became Mayor in 1890, had a music shop at 9-10 Thames Street and for some years had been responsible for putting on a series of concerts which were transferred to the new hall as soon as it was opened.

'*Art is universal*" said Guiseppe Verdi, '*but it is created by individuals*", and what individuals flocked to The Royal Albert Institute At one of the early concerts, Jenny Lind - the 'Swedish Nightingale" - sang and Princess Christian played the piano and sang with '*a soprano voice of pleasing and sweet tone*'. Audiences were to hear her on several future occasions. It was appropriate that she should succeed the Prince Consort as Patron of the Windsor & Eton Choral Society. At another concert on 7th November 1881, conducted by Sir George Elvey, there is an appearance by John S Liddle, ''Soloist and Accompanist'' who was later to acquire fame as the composer of the music to the well-known hymn, '*Abide With Me*".

Between 1884 and 1928, the choir of St George's lured to the Royal Albert Institute conductors such as Sir Walter Parratt, Sir Edward Elgar, Sir Walford Davies, Sydney N Nicholson, organist of Westminster Abbey (who later founded the precursor of the Royal School of Church Music)., an Sir Edward German. Amongst the soloists were

Art is universal

William Booth

Sir Walter Parratt

Dr Charles Macpherson

Sir Walford Davies

several nationally known names. Sir Edward German was the composer of '*Merrie England*' performed by Windsor and Eton Opera in the presence of HRH The Countess of Wessex in 2012 in celebration of the Queen's Diamond Jubilee. The Trust contributed to the costs of this very ambitious production.

At a concert in October 1922, Dr Charles Macpherson, organist of St Paul's Cathedral, conducted some of his own compositions and arrangements. In the following year violin solos were executed by Marie Wilson, who subsequently became leader of the BBC Symphony Orchestra. One of the local musical lions who appeared in The Royal Albert Institute Concerts was Fred Naylor, a St George's legend, who sang alto. He retired in 1959 after sixty two years as a Lay Clerk. He lived to the age of ninety one and his memorial tablet is still to be seen in the Dean's Cloister. Fred Naylor's son, Alec Naylor, was a forerunner of this writer as Captain of the Lay Stewards at St George's Chapel.

Hilaire Belloc

Sir Charles Stanford

General Redvers Buller

A few of the famous visitors to the Royal Albert Institute

Visitors

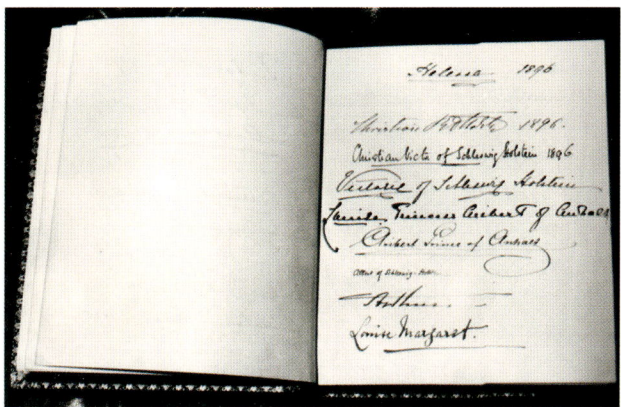

The Royal Albert Institute's Visitors Book showing some of the Royal guests in 1896

The new building was highly regarded by the Royal Family as attested by the signatures in the handsome Visitors' Book, which was saved when the Institute closed and is now part of the Royal Borough Collection. Queen Victoria's signature in 1895 appears as the first in the book and between then and 1902 no less than twenty eight members of the Royal Family inscribed their names therein. These include all seven of the Queen's surviving children, starting with the Prince and Princess of Wales, later King Edward VII and Queen Alexandra, with their son, Prince George and his wife, subsequently George V and Queen Mary, and their daughters, the Princesses Victoria and Maud (afterwards Queen of Norway), Princess Helena with her husband, Prince Christian of Schleswig-Holstein, and their son Prince Christian Victor, who died in the South African War in 1902 and whose fine memorial stands at the foot of the Hundred Steps at the bottom of Thames Street. The other two of Queen Victoria's surviving sons, Prince Alfred, Duke of Edinburgh with his Duchess Marie, and Prince Arthur, Duke of Connaught, together with their sister, Princess Louise, visited on the same day in 1896 and in 1898, Princess Beatrice, the Queen's youngest daughter, came with her own daughter, Victoria Eugenie, afterwards Queen of Spain.

In 1898, the book was signed by the Queen's eldest daughter, '*Victoria Dowager Empress, Frederick Queen of Prussia*'. On a separate occasion,

Visitors

(fortunately) the Royal Albert Institute played host to her son the Kaiser, William Frederick of Prussia and his wife, the Empress Augusta, and shortly afterwards to Prince and Princess Louis of Battenberg (grandparents of HRH The Duke of Edinburgh and parents of Earl Mountbatten of Burma). The last, chronologically, of the British Royal Family in 1901 was Queen Victoria's granddaughter, Princess Alice of Albany, who married the Earl of Athlone, brother to Queen Mary, and whose daughter, Lady May Abel Smith, Queen Victoria's last surviving great grandchild, was a keen supporter of local occasions until her death in 1994.

Victoria Dowager Empress

Marion Terry

Amongst the other celebrities - a term denoting rather more gravitas than it does today - whose signatures adorn the pages of the Visitors' Book are Sir Arthur Sullivan, Fred and Marion Terry, and Edward Spencer Churchill, great uncle of Sir Winston, who lived at Queen's Mead in King's Road and whose widow, Lady Edward, described by Angus Macnaghten as '*undoubtedly the leading personality in the town*', died in a car crash in 1941. Queen's Mead subsequently became the Brigidine Convent and is now the Brigidine School.

Also in the Visitors' Book are the signatures of Sir Charles Stanford, Arthur Bigge Baron Stamfordham (the Queen's Private Secretary), the controversial General Redvers Buller, and William Booth, creator of the Salvation Army for whom, braving heavy rain, the Windsor crowds turned out in force. Hilaire Belloc came in 1915, and the pioneering aviators Brown and Allcock were there in 1919.

Sir Arthur Sullivan

Visitors

Amongst the Windsor notables are recorded the names of Philip Eliot, Dean of Windsor in 1898, and his successor, Albert Baillie, who was President of the Royal Albert Institute from 1929 to 1932. Sir William Carter wrote not only his name but added '*Kt. JP, Alderman, Thirteen times Mayor of Windsor*' - which office he fulfilled between 1902 and 1927 including the whole of the First World War. He was knighted and in 1925 created a Freeman of Windsor for his services to the town. When he and his wife celebrated their Diamond Wedding in 1931, congratulations were sent by the King and Queen, and by the Prince of Wales. To him, when he died in 1932, the Royal Borough is indebted for the bequest of a valuable collection of silver plate.

HRH Prince Philip, the Duke of Edinburgh, Prince Andrew, and Mr Stanley Judd, Chairman of the Trustees, examining the Visitor's Book

Moving Forward

In 1897 the Trustees purchased 5 Park Terrace, Sheet Street which became known as the Royal Albert Institute Annexe, providing much needed additional space.

For sixty years up to the Second World War the fortunes of the Royal Albert Institute flourished exceedingly. For most of the cultural, and indeed other societies in the Town, this was their base. All the productions of the Windsor & Eton Operatic Society were performed there and it was also the venue for a small preparatory school run by a Miss Baillie at which, as a very small boy, the author was for a short time a pupil. A diary belonging to his father contains many entries concerning his membership, starting on 27 September 1916 when, aged 15, he with his friend Ernest Warburton, afterwards a fashionable painter, *'went and joined The Institute'*. The paternal diary reveals attendance in that year at various concerts whilst on Tuesdays there seemed to be regular lectures on such various subjects as the town of Reading, Regimental Reminiscences (by General Carey), the Battle of the Somme, New Zealand, Russia and the Russians, and British Malaya.

On the first anniversary of the Armistice in November 1919, a Miss Akery, who presided over a dancing class to which the author's mother belonged in the Masonic Hall in Church Street, decided to hold a celebratory ball. So successful was this function that a second was held the following year in the main hall of the Institute which memorable event was the scene of the first meeting of the author's parents. Such is fate; as General Gordon observed, *'We are all pianos, events play on us!'*

Between the wars regular Saturday night dances took place in the main hall; a flourishing gym run by Capt. Shardlow, a Sports Master at Eton College, housed another activity. There was also a billiard room and a Royal Albert Institute Tennis Club, the members of which played on courts in the Alexandra Gardens.

Moving Forward

Alexandra Gardens

Susan Mercer recounts in her excellent and evocative history of Windsor Girls' School, several of the school's events between the First and Second World Wars for which the Royal Albert Institute was hired. The first of these historic occasions was held in 1920 the year the school opened, and was

The first Christmas dinner with the second form waiting on the Seniors and a production of 'Arabian Nights' *performed in aid of Holy Trinity Church.*

For the ten years from 1925 to 1935, the Windsor Girls' School Speech Days were held in the Royal Albert Institute and for many years the hall was the scene of well acclaimed and attended dramatic productions of the Old Girls' Association. A popular member of the senior staff, Miss F C (Biddy) Meech, who was a mistress at the school for thirty seven years, produced many of these ambitious plays, with considerable success, and it was most appropriate that in 1975 she herself was appointed a Trustee of the Royal Albert Institute Trust, where her knowledge of music rendered her a valued figure until her death in 1997.

With the outbreak of war in 1939, the benevolent role of The Royal Albert Institute in the life of Windsor and Eton began to diminish. Many of the clubs and societies which were its life blood, shrank or closed. When peace at last came six years later, the decline of the Institute as a force in the cultural vitality of the town accelerated, the buildings began to deteriorate and in 1950 the majority of the premises were let to Berkshire County Council for educational purposes. The spread of television hypnosis reduced the desire for people to seek entertainment outside their own homes, and membership diminished almost to the point of non-existence. Winston Churchill called television a '*bloody harmful invention*'. Certainly, its pervasive infiltration into, and its influence on, all forms of entertainment rendered for The Royal Albert Institute, the coup de grace. As Mr Gilbert Martineau wrote anent the approaching abdication of Charles X of France, '*history was advancing in seven-league boots*'.

A New Vision

The Institute building in the 1960s

At a meeting on 28 April 1966, exactly one hundred years after the first meeting, the Trustees resolved that the buildings should be sold.

This momentous decision could easily have denoted finality for The Royal Albert Institute, but Fate had other plans. It was the legendary Raffles who declared *'we don't alter, Bunny, we only develop'* and so it came about that the original conception of the Founders evolved into the Royal Albert Institute Trust. The Trustees on that historic day of 28 April 1966 were Mr Edmund Luff, Sir Owen Moorshead the Royal Librarian, Mr Egbert Bastow, and the Revd. Ralph Creed-Meredith, former Vicar of Windsor. The long serving Clerk to the Trustees, Mr Cyril Schnadhorst, Senior Partner of Lovegrove & Durant, had died suddenly four months previously and the author was at that meeting, appointed as Clerk in his place.

With the exception of Mr Bastow, the other three Trustees, all of whom by then had retired to the West Country resigned their trusteeships. They were replaced by the election of Alderman Richard Tozer, a past Mayor of Windsor, who became the first Chairman of the new Trust, the Revd. Eric Dawson-Walker, Rector of Holy Trinity, and Messrs F E Thomas and F Shenstone, respectively Manager of the Midland Bank and Managing Director of Pyle Brothers, furnishers in Peascod Street. Mr Thomas Guest and Mr Clement Line who had been associated with the Institute for many years, also became Trustees. Thomas Guest, who died soon afterwards, bequeathed a sum to the Trustees, the income of which was used each year to provide prizes at the Princess Margaret Royal Free School and this bounty continued year by year until the school closed on 31 August 2000.

Richard Tozer

A New Vision

Negotiations intensified over the next few months. Interest from Billy Smart's Circus and the YMCA having proved fruitless, estate agents were instructed. Disposal of the property became ever more urgent with the partial collapse of three ceilings and a spiralling bank overdraft. After numerous meetings throughout 1967 and 1968, the Trustees decided to accept an offer from Daborn Properties Limited for the sum of £36,000. The Charity Commissioners made an Order approving the sale, completion of which on 18 November 1968 was reported to the Trustees at their meeting on 2 December 1968.

In parallel with these negotiations, was the disposal of the Library and various artefacts, as to which the fine collection of books was transferred to the public library. Three oil paintings, including portraits of Queen Victoria and Prince Albert, were sold to the Friends of St George's for £60. The latter now hang in the Vicars' Hall (formerly the Chapter Library) and busts of Mr and Mrs Richardson-Gardner, together with four stained glass windows bearing Royal Coats of Arms, were also presented to the Town.

Following completion of the sale there was left in the Trustees' hands after discharge of the overdraft the capital sum of £25,412.12s, which was invested with the Charity Commission. Only the interest from the capital fund was to be disbursed. The Charity Commission was invited to approve a Scheme under the Charities Act 1960 and this Scheme after considerable wide ranging discussion, including possible alteration of the objects, was sealed by the Commissioners on 10 October 1972, the original 1880 objects being adopted. These were

> *The promotion in Windsor and Eton of the Study of Literature, Science and the Fine Arts and the Delivery of Lectures on subjects of General Interest.*

To this historic formula was added a second paragraph:

> *For the purpose of carrying out the said object the Trustees may make grants to other organisations.*

Although the formalities had of necessity occupied many months, the Trustees were not disposed to delay distribution of the Trust income and at their meeting on 11 March 1969 the first distributions were made. The first, fittingly, was to the Windsor & Eton Society in the sum of £100. The Minute Book records:

A New Vision

Mr Handcock should advise the Secretary that the Society was invited to advance proposals for a specific concert or possibly lecture in memory of the Prince Consort to be suitably named with particular reference to the amount that would be required to put on such a project.

There were nine other recipients:

£200 for the Windsor & Eton Choral Society

£200 for the Windsor & Eton Operatic Society *'this was to be specifically for equipment'*

£100 for the Windsor Arts Society

£50 for Windsor Old Peoples' Welfare Committee *'with a condition that this was to be used for the purpose of its library only'*

£75 for the Workers' Educational Association *'which was to be used specifically for putting on a lecture by a reputable author or scholar'*

£50 for Windsor & Eton Camera Club *'for the specific purpose of purchasing a tape recorder'*

£50 for Windsor Festival Society Limited

£25 for Windsor Parish Players

Seven other applications were refused either as lacking geographical qualification or because their activities fell outside the Trust objects.

The first Royal Albert Institute Trust concert was held at St George's Chapel on 18 April 1970, thereafter the Society has made it, funded by the Trust, an annual fixture in the cultural life of the town; the 2016 concert on 4th June at Cumberland Lodge, is to feature an eminent local Soprano, Rebecca Van den Berg and her internationally renowned accompanist, Marek Ruscyznsky.

By the time of the Trustees' meeting on 5 October 1970, their number was at its full strength, that is to say one ex-officio member, being the Mayor of the Royal Borough of New Windsor (after 1974 the Mayor of the new Royal Borough of Windsor & Maidenhead), and eight elected Trustees. The 1972 Scheme listed the original Trustees as Messrs Tozer, Judd, Line, Shenstone, Thomas, Clibbon, Mackworth-Young (Royal Librarian, later knighted) and the Revd. A Creber, Minister at Windsor Methodist Church.

The Trust

One of the Guildhall's stained glass windows.

The restored drinking fountain outside the Guildhall.

Over the five decades since 1966, regular grants have been made to societies which Prince Albert would undoubtedly have applauded. These include the Royal Windsor Rose & Horticultural Society (which each year presents at its annual show the Royal Albert Institute Shield), the Windsor Festival, the Rotary Club of Windsor & Eton for the annual Youth Speaks Competition, Windsor & Eton Operatic Society, Windsor Theatre Guild, Windsor Fringe, Windsor Arts Centre, Windsor Local History Publications Group, The Royal Free Singers, the Royal Borough Youth Orchestra, the Windsor Theatre Describers Association, and the Friends of the Royal Borough Museum. Local schools in particular have received donations of musical instruments and funding for various of their activities.

Other more exotic benefactions, but still firmly within the Trust Objects, have embraced the renovation of the exceptionally fine tomb of Idonea Audley, Abbess of Burnham, in the Parish Church burial ground, a presentation plate commemorating the St George's Chapel Quincentenary to the Guildhall, renovation of the drinking fountain at the Guildhall and of the George V Memorial in Datchet Road, presentation of a portrait of Queen Anne to Princess Margaret Royal Free School, now removed to the St Edwards Ecumenical School, together with an enlarged photograph of the stained glass window depicting that king in the West Window of St George's Chapel. A further picture of Queen Anne was donated to Queen Anne First School. Payments have also been made for the repainting of the armorial bearings on the Victoria

The Trust

Street Alms Houses, for the telescope installed by the Herschel Astronomical Society in the grounds of Eton College, and towards the restoration of the organs in the Parish and All Saints Churches. Amongst literary works by local authors supported by grants or underwriting, have been:

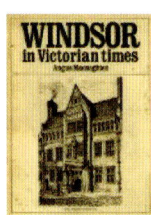

Windsor in Victorian Times
by Angus Macnaghten

In the Midst of the People
by Valerie Bonham

Writers in Windsor
by Hester Davenport

In Service to Three Monarchs at Windsor
by Norman Oxley

The Harcourt Journals and St Leonard's Hill
by Pat and Sheila Rooney

Royal Windsor - Images of a Bygone Age
by Elias Kupfermann

The annual Bond Lectures given in St George's Chapel in memory of Maurice Bond, MVO, amongst other appointments Honorary Archivist to the Royal Borough of Windsor and Clerk of the Records at the House of Lords, and respected Windsor author, and his wife Shelagh, have been intermittently financially supported for some years. The Band of the Windsor Sea Cadets, Training Ship Windsor Castle, the restoration of the Eton Cattle Pound, and the restoration of Boehm's statue of Queen Victoria, unveiled on Castle Hill on 22 June 1887 to celebrate Her Majesty's Golden Jubilee, have also benefitted from the Trust's liberality.

On 3 January 1988, following the New Year's service at the Parish Church, the Trust presented to the town a portrait of King William IV by Mr Theodore Ramos which now hangs in the Guildhall Chamber. As part of the celebrations of the Queen's Golden Jubilee, Her Majesty unveiled a new portrait of herself, also by Theodore Ramos, at the Guildhall on 3 June 2002, and this now hangs in the Ascot Room. The Queen consented to wear for this picture a piece of the Royal Jewellery known as *The Albert Brooch*, given to Queen Victoria by Prince Albert on their wedding day on 10 February 1840. This brooch is indeed a splendid piece and is described in Cecil Woodham Smith's *Queen*

The Trust

The Albert Brooch

Victoria 1819-1861, as '*a superb brooch of an immense sapphire set round with diamonds*' and, as if that was not enough, as '*magnificent*'.

From time to time, the possibility of widening the Trust Objects has been suggested but this notion has never found favour with the Trustees. At a meeting on 16 February 1971, this policy went far to being vindicated when the Mayor, Kit Aston, later Sir Christopher Aston, outlined his ideas for the creation of a "*parallel Trust*" which would cover the larger area of the Royal Borough of Windsor & Maidenhead, but with wider objects, including sporting activities. He hoped that it would be sponsored by His Royal Highness The Duke of Edinburgh, and Aston added that he felt the inception of the new Trust was '*as a direct result of his Trusteeship of the Royal Albert Institute*". The Prince Philip Trust for the Royal Borough of Windsor & Maidenhead, set up in 1977 with the Royal Albert Institute's Scheme as its prototype, today flourishes with a capital of over £1,500,000. (Unlike The Prince Philip Trust, the Royal Albert Institute does not engage in active fund-raising.) The author became its first Secretary/Trustee and served in that capacity for the first twenty five years.

In due course, the old Royal Albert Institute buildings were demolished, and on 30 October 1978 the Duke of Edinburgh visited the new building erected on the site, then occupied by the Windsor Life Assurance Company, to view the two restored statues of the Prince Consort. Messrs Judd, Clibbon and Handcock, Chairman, Vice Chairman and Clerk respectively, and Sir Robin Mackworth-Young, Trustee, were presented to His Royal Highness, together with Mr J H Gough who had restored the statues. Prince Philip presented the Mayor with the original Visitors' Book which as its final entry carries the following inscription:

> *This Visitors' Book was presented, at the request and in the presence of, the under-mentioned Trustees of the Royal Albert Institute Trust, for permanent exhibition at the Guildhall Windsor by His Royal Highness, the Prince Philip Duke of Edinburgh, KG, KT to Councillor N Whiteley, Mayor of the Royal Borough of Windsor & Maidenhead on the occasion of His Royal Highness's visit to Royal Albert House, Windsor on 30 October 1978.*'

The Trust

The Visitors' Book was actually placed on view in the Madam Tussaud's Exhibition at the Great Western Railway Station until that venture closed, when the book was returned to the custody of the Local Authority.

The importance of books and the reading of books had ever been uppermost in the Trustees' contemplation. They would have concurred with the late Somerset Maugham in his reflection,

> *when I look back on my long life, I realise reading has been one of the most enduring pleasures life has offered me.*

It was in this frame of mind that in February 1985 the Trustees considered an application from Mr John Townsend, Headmaster of the Princess Margaret Royal Free School, which had been offered a collection of twenty two books previously belonging to the late Thomas Edward Luff for the sum of £ 700, the estimated value of which was £875. Thomas Luff, Mayor of Windsor in 1912, was a member of a well known family of Windsor stationers and his collection comprised much local history. The school undertook that the collection would be available for pupils, teachers and interested members of the public for the benefit of future generations of students of local history. The Trustees in the event purchased the collection and spent a further £ 109.50 on repairing two of the volumes. The Luff Library was opened on 15 May 1985 by Mr Peter Luff, MP for Worcester and Thomas Luff's grandson, in the presence of representatives of the school and of the Trustees. When the school closed the collection was transferred to Windsor Public Library, where the librarian confirms that it is '*well used*'.

In February 1992, the Trustees had a further and even more important opportunity to demonstrate their bibliophilia when a grant of £1,500 enabled the Royal Borough Collection to purchase a collection of books, prints, lithographs, paintings and other documents, almost all concerned with Windsor, which had been amassed over many years by Mr Patrick Manley and which had been offered to the Borough at a greatly reduced price. Mrs Judith Hunter of the Royal Borough Collection wrote:

> *to record our very grateful thanks to the Royal Albert Institute Trust for this benefaction which had enabled this important collection to be preserved intact in safe hands.*

The Trust

As long before the event as the Trustees' meeting on 12 June 1995, the Minutes record that the author, as Clerk to the Trustees, suggested that

> *looking ahead to the Millennium in five years time the Trustees might like to consider putting by funds annually towards a specific purpose within the Trust objects.*

The Trustees adopted this idea with enthusiasm and over the next four meetings the nature of such a focussed bounty for the town was vigorously debated at considerable length. At the meeting on 18 November 1996 there were four proposals on the table, one of which, promoted with enterprising energy by one of the Trustees, Mr F E Shenstone MBE, was an ambitious plan to replace and then reorganise the choir stalls in the Chancel of Windsor Parish Church. This scheme, favoured by the rector, the Revd Jeffrey Whale, was designed to enable the church, in the face of falling congregations, to be used more regularly for concerts and thus to preserve its viability for future generations. The minutes record that '*the Trustees were minded to accept the Parish Church proposals subject to qualifications*', one of which was that they should have an opportunity of attending the church with the architect, which they in fact did on 21 February 1997. At their meeting the following month they resolved that '*the Parish Church theme was acceptable in principle subject to full details of the proposals*'. The rector subsequently attended a Trustees' meeting to explain outstanding points, and at their meeting on 29 June 1998 Mr Shenstone reported that the work was proceeding. It was secure in that knowledge that shortly afterwards he passed away and at their meeting in November, the Trustees stood in his memory. On 15 November 1999 payment of the grant of £10,000 was authorised for this Millennium project which was then the largest donation ever made by the Trustees. A plaque recording the Trust's grant was to be affixed to the new installation, although in truth, it might easily also have recorded

WIndsor Parish Church

The Trust

the fruition of the late Freddie Shenstone's commitment and perseverance in bringing about this project of considerable benefit to the musical life of the town. His daughter, Christine Heybourn, is currently a Sidesman at the Church.

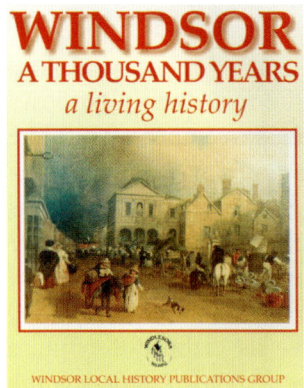

Often, when considering applications for financial help from local authors on local topics, the Trustees offer a loan rather than a grant, repayment to depend on the plentitude or otherwise of sales. One regular applicant dealt with in this way is the Windsor Local History Group in respect of their occasional publications. One such is the Group's publication in 2001 of a brilliantly researched and carefully constructed *Windsor, A Thousand Years of Living History* which received a loan of £500. The book rapidly sold out and went almost immediately into the first of two reprints. As with all these loans to the Group, this one was speedily repaid.

In 2002 the Trustees embarked on another imaginative project to celebrate the Queen's Golden Jubilee in addition to the presentation of the new portrait of Her Majesty to the Guildhall. In so doing they drew the Trust firmly into the twenty first century by the purchase and distribution to each of the twenty schools in Windsor and Eton of a Microsoft Encarta Reference Library on four CD-ROMS incorporating the Encarta Encyclopedia. Given his intense interest in all things scientific, Prince Albert would undoubtedly have been at the forefront of the Information Technology revolution, and this Golden Jubilee gift to the local schools was a venture which he would have readily endorsed. When planning Imperial College in Kensington in 1851, he observed:

progress is to be obtained in human knowledge by (inter alia) personal study from books and oral communication of knowledge to those who wish to acquire it

In so far as such knowledge could be furthered by modern means, his support would have been unqualified.

The Queen's Golden Jubilee was celebrated throughout the country no more enthusiastically than in the Royal County of Berkshire. An imaginative

The Trust

project entitled '*Golden Youth*" was promulgated by the Lord Lieutenant for the Royal County of Berkshire, Mr Philip Wroughton, and on 10 May 2002 the event took place at Bisham Abbey, where The Queen and the Duke of Edinburgh watched a multitude of displays by groups of the 2,000 children attending the gathering. An application to the Trustees for funding highlighted the dilemma in which the Trustees occasionally find themselves. The Trust instrument of 1972 specifies the area of benefit as '*Windsor in the Royal County of Berkshire and Eton in the County of Buckingham*", these locations being prior to the redrawing of many county and town boundaries which saw the ancient Royal Borough of New Windsor and Eton Town swallowed by the Royal Borough of Windsor and Maidenhead. It was the former locations that fall within the Trust's bounty. When faced with a proposal involving persons or organisations beyond these boundaries, an enquiry is put in hand to ascertain the percentage of participants who qualify under the Trust's regulations. In the case of Golden Youth a fair number of the children were able to claim geographical qualification.

Another constraint on the Trust's powers naturally relates to the purpose of the contribution required; thus applications having as their object sports activities, or relating to health problems, are beyond the Trust's remit. Often, however, it is possible to assist such institutions as the local Scout and Guide movement or the King George VI Day Centre in Clarence Road with grants for books and other reading or teaching material.

Memories of Charles Knight, founder of the Windsor and Eton Express, were kindled when in 2004 the Friends of the Royal Borough Museum were granted £500 towards the purchase of two water colours of Knight and his wife, painted by John Callington Moore in 1874. Both pictures now hang in the Guildhall. Ten years later, on 1 August 2014, the Windsor Local History Group marked the two hundredth anniversary of the newspaper with the publication of a new book entitled *Windsor and Eton Express, 1812-1830, the Charles Knight Years* for which a loan of £500 (since repaid) was made. This for Windsor, was an exceptionally worthy venture. The preface noted:

> *For this exemplary book, Windsor Local History Group is to be congratulated: it is a valuable and intriguing excursion into our history two hundred years ago, seen through the pages of the town's very own newspaper.*

The Trust

In 2006, the Trustees brought forward their summer meeting to 28 April in order to celebrate the fortieth anniversary of the reconstructed Trust on 28 April 1966. It was an appropriate occasion to note that the author's *'definitive history of The Royal Albert Institute and Trust had been completed and copies distributed to the Trustees'*.

It is perhaps worth recording the eight successful applications before the Trust on that fortieth anniversary, each one a not untypical example of the Trust's benevolence. Two went towards the cost of concerts:

£750 to Windsor Festival towards the Berkshire Young Musician's Trust concert

£250 was awarded in respect of a Mozart concert by Cafe Mozart in the Dungeon at Windsor Castle

£400 was granted to the Royal Windsor Rose and Horticultural Society for the popular ''Busy Lizzie Plant Competition'' for schools, together with prizes accompanying the Royal Albert Institute Shield and the Lady Hannon Cup

£60 was given to the imminently closing Eton Wick and Boveney Women's Institute to cover the costs of a scrapbook covering the last twenty two years of the Institute's history up to 4 January 2006.

A guarantee was provided to Windsor Theatre Guild in the sum of £1,000 to cover any possible loss on a forthcoming production of *'Tom Jones"* in the Chapter Gardens at Windsor Castle; and sums of £200, £350, and £250 were respectively granted to the 12th Windsor Scouts, Windsor Fringe and Dedworth Middle School for books and prizes.

At this time it was reported that the annual grants and guarantees awarded over the year's three meetings amounted to a total of £7,460 distributed between twenty two applicants.

It may be thought that these are not very substantial figures, as to which there are two answers. Firstly, however modest the grant may appear, it is very often the actual amount sought. Secondly, the Trustees consciously husband their resources to enable a much larger outlay to be made when the occasion demands. It is, in any event, axiomatic; whether large or small, the disbursements are invariably of significant help to the applicants and, judged

The Trust

by their letters of appreciation, provide a timely stimulation to numerous worthwhile cultural activities in Windsor and Eton.

The fortieth anniversary was regarded to be of sufficient recognition as to justify a minor flourish of trumpets. The minutes record:

> *after the meeting, the Trustees celebrated the fortieth anniversary with champagne and delicacies for the preparation of which the three lady Trustees were warmly thanked.*

(It should be noted that the refreshments were not funded by theTrust!)

At the meeting on 6 June 2007, the minutes record that the Trustees were invited

> *To consider the possibility of funding some project in Windsor and Eton to mark the Diamond Wedding of The Queen and the Duke of Edinburgh on 20 November 2007.*

This event by any criteria would be a remarkable anniversary. The Trustees were enjoined to bring forward suggestions at the next meeting. At the next meeting on 14 November the Mayor, Cllr Leo Walters,

> *mentioned that approval had been obtained from the Deputy Ranger, Mr Philip Everett, for the planting of an oak tree in the Great Park on behalf of the Royal Borough. Mr Handcock was requested to communicate with Mr Everett to ascertain the cost and practicality of a similar gift.*

The Deputy Ranger's co-operation was, in fact, forthcoming. A letter to the Queen's Private Secretary sought Her Majesty's permission, which continued in a spirit of optimism:

> *If the above meets with approval, the Trustees would be honoured and delighted should a Royal Planting be possible at some convenient time.*

It was with immense gratification that a few days later Mr Handcock received a telephone call from the Palace to the effect that the Queen had not only given her permission but would plant the tree herself. In consequence, on a Sunday morning the following April, after attending Mattins in the Royal Chapel in the Great Park, the Queen, accompanied by the Duke of York, after presentation of the Trustees, symbolically, and with charm and humour, planted an English

The Trust

Her Majesty Queen Elizabeth II

Her Majesty Queen Elizabeth II with the author, Mr John Handcock

Oak. The tree is situated a short distance into the Deer Park, close to Royal Lodge. A plaque bears the following inscription:

Presented to H M The Queen and H R H The Duke of Edinburgh by The Royal Albert Institute Trust to mark their Diamond Wedding on 20th November 2007 and planted by Her Majesty on 20 April 2008.

In his book *A Family Album*, the late Duke of Windsor wrote:

To the south spreads the spacious Great Park, with the Long Walk stretching three miles through the soft green English landscape and the meadows of the Home Park to the south, refreshed by the waters of the slowly winding Thames.

The Trustees took much delight in adding a small contribution to the splendours of The Great Park.

L to R: Bill Cathcart, Leo Walter (Mayor), Peter Gray MBE (Chairman), Colin Oakley, Bill Cooley JP, Joyce Sampson, Douglas Hill, Rosemary Ussher

In 2009, it was the turn of the Windsor Theatre Guild to chalk up a notable birthday when, to signal the company's seventy years, a finely produced

The Trust

book was published, *Windsor Theatre Guild, A Celebration 1939-2009*. The Guild has received financial support over the years for its excellent productions, including an underwriting of £1,000 in respect of the company's production in July 2009 of *The Canterbury Tales* subsequently switched to *King Lear*. The Trustees provided an underwriting of £500 for publication of the book.

A peripheral matter which occupied the Trustees over four or five meetings in 2008 and 2009 derived from an offer by a Mr Hughes of two silver cups won by his father, a member of the Institute for billiards and snooker respectively. Both cups carried plaques recording the winners, the former between 1914 and 1953 and the latter between 1934 and 1953. A previous winner was Egbert Bastow, who had been a Trustee at the commencement of the Trust in its new form in 1966 as recounted earlier. Generous although the offer was, the Trustees possessed no facilities to display the cups. Negotiations with the Local Authority concluded happily when they were accepted by the Royal Borough Museum which would '*be happy to display the cups on behalf of the Museum in the display case at the Windsor Guildhall*' where they now repose.

At the Trustees' meeting on 10 June 2010, it was noted that in 2012 the Queen would celebrate her Diamond Jubilee and the Chairman asked the Trustees '*to give some thought as to what the Trust might do*'. At the next meeting it was reported that the Windsor and Eton Society was also canvassing suggestions '*for a suitable way to mark this prestigious event*'. Mrs Ussher, a Trustee, propounded a suggestion that the Trust might like to put forward to the Diamond Jubilee Steering Committee that a one and a half sized sculpture of a pair of Windsor Greys be commissioned to be placed on an elevated plinth on the roundabout at the junction of Osborne Road and Kings Road. It was agreed that this proposal should be supported and if it was accepted by the Steering Committee they would consider a substantial donation towards the costs.

The Windsor and Eton Society ultimately received over forty suggestions from the general public, from which a short-list of ten had been selected. These ten, however, did not include the equine sculpture. At a meeting on 8 June 2011 the Trustees considered an application by the Windsor and Eton Society for financial support for the winner of its competition. This was to be a sculpture of contemporary design described by one Trustee as '*resembling a molecular diagram from a science text book with no regal or diamond connotation'*. This choice was rejected by the Trustees. Mr Handcock was asked to investigate the ideas of the runner-up in the Society's competition. At the November meeting of 2011, it was reported that as one of the proposals made to the Windsor and Eton Society in their competition for a suitable commemorative tribute, Mrs Hester Davenport, Chairman of the Windsor Local History Group, had

> *proposed the commissioning and installation of a commemorative stained glass window for installation in the Guildhall.*

In the event, after discussions with the Local Authority and English Heritage, the Trust commissioned Artemis Glass of Staines to proceed with the creation of two stained glass windows for the Ascot Room to a design approved by the Trustees. The design which emerged involved four roundels, two in each window, depicting the four Royal Palaces, Buckingham Palace, Windsor Castle, Sandringham, and Balmoral. The other embellishments which enhanced the windows included representations in the four corners of each window of the Albert Brooch, previously described as worn by the Queen in her Golden Jubilee portrait. Artemis Glass proceeded with the work and when, at the invitation of the Mayor, the Trustees met in the Ascot Room of the Guildhall on 14 November 2012, the newly installed stained glass windows were there for the Trustees to see and *'general admiration and approval was unanimously expressed'*.

The total cost of the windows amounted to £ 9,910. Various peripheral costs took it to around £11, 000 the largest single grant in the history of the Trust. In addition, the Trustees were able to donate £ 5,000 payable over two years to the Windsor Greys appeal. The Trustees next turned their attention to a ceremonial dedication of the windows. Correspondence ensued with the Queen's Private Secretary and on 14 June, Sir Christopher Geidt wrote to Mr Handcock,

> *I refer to our exchange of correspondence about the possibility of The Queen visiting The Guildhall at Windsor for the dedication of the pair of stained glass windows which the Royal Albert Institute has commissioned to commemorate Her Majesty's Diamond Jubilee. The Queen has now taken decisions on her programme for the remainder of this year and I am pleased to inform you that she would be delighted to visit The Guildhall on the morning of Friday 29 November.*

The Trust

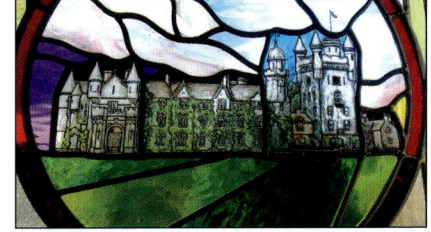

The Diamond Jubilee Windows

The Trust

The occasion was, indeed, a very happy one with all the Trustees and the Clerk being presented to Her Majesty. In the course of the ceremony Her Majesty was presented with a copy of the first edition of *The Institute that Became an Institution* which had been bound in leather and bore the inscription:

> *This short Monograph was presented to Her Majesty Queen Elizabeth II by The Royal Albert Institute Trust on the 29* day of November 2013 as a Memento of Her Majesty's dedication of a pair of stained glass windows in the Ascot Room in the Guildhall at Windsor in commemoration of Her Majesty's Diamond Jubilee.*

The Queen thereafter unveiled a brass plaque which read:

> *This pair of stained glass windows, crafted by Artemis Glass of Staines, was commissioned and presented by the Royal Albert Institute Trust to commemorate the Diamond Jubilee of H M The Queen and this plaque was unveiled by Her Majesty on 29 November 2013 in the presence of His Royal Highness The Duke of Edinburgh and of the Trustees.*
>
> *Mr Peter Gray MBE, Chairman, Mr J E Handcock CVO, DL Clerk to the Trustees*

As a footnote, it gives the greatest satisfaction to record that the funding needed for the sculpture of the pair of Windsor Greys was raised in no small measure by reason of the Duke of Cambridge becoming Patron of the Appeal and this handsome sculpture, which was unveiled by the Queen on 30 March 2014, may be viewed on the roundabout at the junction of Osborne Road and Kings Road. The Minutes of 11 June 2014 record:

> *Warm congratulations were offered to Mrs Ussher in respect of the completion of the statues of The Queen's horses...Doubts as to whether Mrs Ussher would be able to raise the requisite monies had been triumphantly assuaged.*

The Trust

The Windsor Greys

Daniel and Storm

Sculpted by

Robert Rattray

Into and Beyond the 21st Century

To this day the Trustees' meetings have taken place regularly at only four venues. For the first thirty five years they were held at the offices of the solicitors Lovegrove & Durant in Park Street. Since 2004, with the removal of the firm to Frances Road, they were, by agreement with the then partners, held at these latter premises on the site of the old Corby Trouser Press factory which was even earlier the home of the Brown family's carriage business.

Since 2010 the Trustees have met at the Ellison House Alms Houses in Victoria Street, and latterly at The Local Authority premises, York House in Sheet Street. Occasionally, at the invitation of the Mayor, meetings have been held in the Ascot Room of The Guildhall, under the watchful eye of her Majesty in her Golden Jubilee portrait. In these years there have been only four Chairmen, Messrs Richard Tozer, Stanley Judd, Ronald Clibbon DL, and the present incumbent, Peter Gray MBE. The current Trustees, in addition to the Chairman and the Mayor for the time being, who is ex officio, are Douglas Hill, former Mayor of Eton, and Vice Chairman, Colin Oakley, the Treasurer, Mr Brian Hoare, Lady Palmer, now Mrs Palmer-Scott, and Mesdames Joyce Sampson, Rosemary Ussher, and Penny Branch. The author continues as Clerk to the Trustees.

The Trust's finances are commendably healthy: the opening capital sum of £25,412.12s has, with careful management, grown as recorded at the 2014 AGM to some £285,000 and every year most applications for funding from a variety of organisations falling within the 1880 area and objects, receive favourable response from the Trustees.

As Miss Lucy Norton records in her book *The Sun King and His Loves*, it was the conviction of Louis XIV that *'great enterprises are bound to succeed if the details are carefully enough considered'*. A more succinct aphorism emanated from King Leopold I of the Belgians, uncle both to Queen Victoria and Prince Albert. *'The great thing is success,'* said he. Over the generations it is on the solid basis of the painstaking attention by its adherents to the mass of details surrounding the concept of the Royal Albert Institute that its amazing success has evolved and flourished.

Into and Beyond the 21st Century

The spirit of Francis Charles Augustus Albert Emmanuel, Prince of Saxe-Coburg and Gotha, The Prince Consort lives on, and indubitably Queen Victoria would have been more than amused; she would have been enraptured!

Appendix

Names of the Trustees appointed since 28 April 1960:

Alderman R H Tozer, JP Chairman	Mr R South
Mr Joseph Martyn, MA	Cllr W G Cooley, JP
The Reverend E Dawson-Walker	Mr P Gray, MBE (Chairman)
Mr F E Thomas, JP	Mr C Oakley
Mr C J B Line	Mr G Heape
Mr F C Shenstone, MBE	Mr I Garnham
Mr R J Clibbon, DL JP (Chairman)	Mrs J Sampson
Mr S E R Judd, JP' (Chairman)	Mrs R Ussher
Sir Robin Mackworth-Young KCVO	Mrs P Branch
The Reverend A Creber	Mr B Hoare
Canon D N Griffiths	Cllr D Hill
Miss F C Meech	Lady Palmer
Cllr R E Shaw, DL	

From 1966, each successive Mayor of the Royal Borough of New Windsor served as a Trustee during his or her period of Office. From 1974 the Mayors of the Royal Borough of Windsor and Maidenhead have served in a similar fashion.

Bibliography

M Bond, MVO OBE	*The Story of Windsor*
The Community of St John the Baptist Clewer	*The Founders of Clewer*
E H Fellowes, MVO MA Mus.Doc	*The Knights of the Garter 1348 - 1939*
The Graphic Magazine	
C Hibbert	*Edward VII*
Illustrated London News	*The Opening of the Royal Albert Institute, Sheet Street, Windsor*
A Macnaughton	*Windsor in Victorian Times*
Marshall's Guide to Windsor	
S Mercer	*Girls in Green, Windsor Girls' School 1920-2005*
A T Pinder	*St George's Choir and the Royal Albert Institute. Report of the Society of the Friends of St George's and the Descendents of the Knights of the Garter 1977-1978*
Royal Borough Museum Collection	*Visitors' Book of the Royal Albert Institute*
Trustees of the Royal Albert Institute Trust	*Minutes of Meetings 1966-2014*
A N Wilson	*The Victorians*
Windsor Local History Group	*Windsor: A Thousand Years of Living History*
C Woodham-Smith	*Queen Victoria, Her Life and Times 1819-1861*

Index of People

A

Akery, Miss 12
Albert, Prince Consort 2, 3, 7, 15, 18, 22, 32, 33
Alcock, Sir John 10
Alexander, Earl of Atlone 10
Alexandra, Princess of Wales, (later Queen Alexandra) 9
Alfred, Prince, Duke of Edinburgh 9
Alice, Princess, Countess of Athlone 10
Andrew, Prince, Duke of York 11, 25
Anne, Queen 17
Arthur, Prince, Duke of Connaught 9
Aston, Sir Christopher 19
Augusta, Empress 10

B

Bacon, H F 4
Baillie, Albert, Dean of Winsor 11,
Baillie, Miss 12
Bastow, Egbert 14, 27
Beatrice, Princess Henry of Battenburg 9
Bell, E Ingress 4
Belloc, Hilaire 8, 10
Boehm, Sir J E, Bart
Bond, Maurice 18
Bond, Shelagh 18
Bonham, Revd Valerie 18
Booth, William 8, 10
Branch, Penny 32, 34
Brown, Sir Arthur 10
Buckland, Frank 3
Bulkeley, Captain 6
Buller, General Redvers 8, 10

C

Carey, General 12
Carter, Sir William 11

Charles X, King of France 13
Christian, Prince of Schleswig-Holstein 3, 6, 9
Christian Victor, Prince of Schleswig-Holstein 9
Churchill, Lord Edward Spencer 10
Churchill, Lady Edward Spencer 10
Churchill, Sir Winston Spencer 3, 10, 13
Clibbon, Ronald J, DL, JP 16, 32, 34
Cooley, William G, JP 34
Creber, Revd. A 16, 34
Creed-Meredith, Revd. Ralph 14

D

Davenport, Hester 18, 28
Davies, Sir Walford 7
Dawson-Walker, Revd. Eric 14, 34
Dempsey, Glen
den Berg, Rebecca Van 16
Drew, Mr 6
Dyson, Thomas 7

E

Edward, Prince of Wales, (later King Edward VIII)
Edward, Prince of Wales (later KingEdward VII) 4, 6, 9
Edward, the Confessor, King and Saint
Elgar, Sir Edward 7
Eliot, Philip, Dean of Windsor 10
Elizabeth II, Queen 18, 22, 23, 25, 26, 27, 28, 30
Elvey, Sir George 6, 7
Everett, Philip 25

F

Fairbank, Dr 6

G

Garnham, John
Geit, Sir Christopher, KCVO, OBE 26
George, Prince of Wales (later King
    George V) 9, 17
George VI, King 23
German, Sir Edward 7
Gordon, General 12
Gough, J H 4, 19
Gray, Peter, MBE 26, 30, 32, 34
Griffith, Revd Canon D N 34
Guest, Thomas 14

H

Handcock, Eric
Handcock, Gladys
Handcock, John E, CVO, DL, 12, 16,
    19, 21, 25, 26, 28, 30, 32,
Hannon, Lady
Heape, Mr G 34
Helena Victoria, Princess Christian of
    Schleswig-Holstein 7, 9
Heybourn, Christine 22
Hill, Douglas 32, 34
Hoare, Brian 32, 34
Hughes, Mr 27
Hunter, Judith 20

I

Idonea Audley, Abbess of Burnham 17

J

Judd, Stanley E R, JP 16, 19, 32, 34

K

Knight, Charles 23
Kupfermann, Elias 18

L

Leopold I of the Belgians, King 32
Liddle, John S 7
Lind, Jenny 7
Line, Clement 14, 16, 34
Louis XIV, King of France
Louis, Mountbatten, Earl of Burma
Louis, Prince of Battenburg 10
Louise, Princess, Duchess of Fife 9
Luff, Edmund 14
Luff, Peter, MP 20
Luff, Thomas Edward 20

M

Mackarness, Rt. Revd. John, Bishop of
    Oxford 6
Mackworth-Young, Sir Robin, KCVO
    16, 19, 34
Macnaghten, Angus 10, 18
Macpherson, Dr Charles 8
Manley, Patrick, MVO 20
Marie, Princess, Duchess of Edinburgh,
    9
Martineau, Gilbert 13
Martyn, Joseph, MA 34
Mary, Princess of Wales (later Queen
    Mary) 9
Maud, Princess (later Queen of Norway)
    9
Maugham, Somerset 20
Meech, Miss F C 13, 34
Mercer, Susan 13
Moore, John Callington 23
Moorshead, Sir Owen 14

N

Naylor, Alec 8
Naylor, Fred 8
Nicholson, Sydney N 7

Index of People

Norton, Lucy 32

O

Oakley, Colin 26, 32, 34
Oxley, Norman 18

P

Palmer-Scott, Joanna 32, 34
Parratt, Sir Walter 7
Philip, Prince, The Duke of Edinburgh, 10, 11, 19, 28, 25

R

Ramos, Theodore 18
Rattray, Robert 31
Rawlins, Revd. R G 6
Richardson-Gardner, Mr R 6, 15
Richardson-Gardner, Mrs R 4, 15
Romanelli, Signor 4
Rooney, Pat 18
Rooney, Sheila 18
Ruscyznsky, Marek 16

S

Sampson, Joyce 26, 32, 34
Schnadhorst, Cyril 14
Shardlow, Captain Henry 12
Shaw, R E, DL 34
Shenstone, F E, MBE 14, 16, 21, 22, 34
Smart, Billy
Smith, Lady May Abel 10
Sophie, Countess of Wessex 7
South, Raymond 34
Stamfordham, Baron Arthur Bigge 10
Stanford, Sir Charles 8, 10
Sullivan, Sir Arthur 10

T

Terry, Fred 10
Terry, Marion 10
Thomas, Frank E 14, 16, 34
Townsend, John 20
Tozer, Richard 14, 16, 32, 34
Tussaud, Mme Marie 20

U

Ussher, Rosemary 26, 27, 30, 32, 34

V

Verdi, Guiseppe
Victoria, Dowager Empress Frederick, Queen of Prussia 9
Victoria, Princess Louis of Battenburg 9, 10
Victoria Eugenie, Princess (later Queen of Spain) 9
Victoria, Queen 2, 9, 10, 15, 18, 32, 33

W

Walters, Leo 25, 26
Warburton, Ernest 12
Webb, John 6
Wellesley, The Hon. and Very Revd. Gerald, Dean of Windsor 6
Whale, Revd Jeffrey 21
Whiteley, Neville 19
William IV, King 18
William Frederick, King of Prussia 10
William, Prince, Duke of Cambridge 30
Wilson, Mr A N 3
Wilson, Marie 8
Woodham-Smith, Cecil
Wroughton, Philip (later Sir Philip Wroughton KCVO) 23